LEARNING THE RECORDER

LEARNING THE RECORDER

NANCY MARTIN L.R.S.M.

Senior Lecturer in Music
Victoria University of Wellington
Department of University Extension

FREDERICK WARNE & CO LTD
London · New York

Published in Great Britain by
Frederick Warne & Co Ltd
London
1970

Reprinted 1971

ISBN Limp Edition 0 7232 1126 4
ISBN Full Bound Edition 0 7232 1280 5

Printed in Great Britain by
Lowe & Brydone (Printers) Ltd., London

Contents

★

PART ONE

PART TWO

Foreword

★

The recorder was one of the most popular musical instruments in the 16th, 17th and 18th centuries. Henry VIII played recorders and owned seventy-six of them. Samuel Pepys wrote in his diary in 1667, 'did buy a recorder, which I do intend to learn to play on, the sound of it being, of all sounds in the world, most pleasing to me'. Many composers in Italy, France, Germany and England, including Bach and Handel, composed works specially for the recorder. In the 18th century, it was gradually replaced by the transverse flute which has a bigger range and a more powerful tone. The recorder was revived in this century by men such as Arnold Dolmetsch, and today a number of modern composers are writing music for recorders.

The special advantage of the recorder is that, unlike the modern flute, it is easy to blow so that one can make music on it in the first lesson. But, like any other musical instrument, the recorder requires a lot of practice to play it really well. It is hoped that many who begin learning the recorder from this book will persevere and will enjoy playing with others the music that is available at all grades of difficulty from various publishers.

Playing the recorder is strongly recommended by many educational authorities. To help teachers, Miss Nancy Martin conducted many classes and tried out various ways of teaching it. She soon found that teaching the recorder involved teaching incidentally a good deal of the simple grammar of music. Her methods were so successful that there was a demand for duplicated notes and tunes which could be followed by those who could not attend her classes. In writing this book Miss Martin has revised these notes in the light of experience and has added to them considerably. *Learning the Recorder* is written primarily for schools so that every pupil may have a copy of the tunes and be able to progress at his or her own rate. It is equally useful, however, for the adult who wishes to learn something about music through playing a simple instrument.

ACKNOWLEDGEMENT

The publishers wish to thank the following for their kind permission to reproduce music: Messrs. J. B. Cramer & Co. Ltd., London, for 'Skye Boat Song' on page 42; Messrs. Schott & Co. Ltd., London, for the tables of fingering on pages 78 and 79.

Part One

★

THE INSTRUMENT

The recorder is an instrument of the flute family. It differs from the transverse flute used in the modern orchestra in that it is played by blowing directly into the mouthpiece as in playing the clarinet. Blockflöte is the German name for the recorder, and some German recorders have a slightly different system of fingering.

Recorders are made in five sizes: the descant and tenor in the key of C and the sopranino, the treble and bass in the key of F. Those in most common use are the descant, treble, and tenor. The bass and the sopranino are used mainly in consort playing. As the fingering of all the instruments is alike, anyone who has learned to play both a C and an F instrument can play all five.

Range

Recorders, other than the bass, have just over a two octave range.

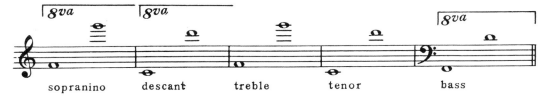

The sopranino, the descant and the bass sound one octave higher than the written note, but to avoid many leger lines it is convenient to write the music at the same pitch as for the treble and tenor recorders. The bass clef is used for the bass recorder. Most bass recorders have less than a two octave range, but the Dolmetsch bass recorder has the full two octaves.

Tuning

Recorders are tuned to standard pitch (A-440), but the pitch can be lowered by pulling out the mouthpiece from the barrel of the recorder. This should be done with a screwing movement. If recorders are to be used with the piano, it is necessary to see that the piano is tuned to the correct pitch.

BUYING A RECORDER

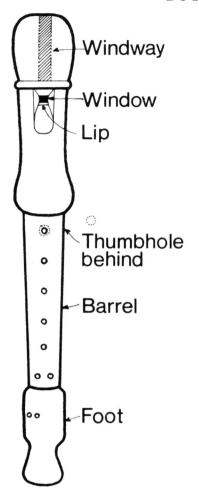

Windway

Window

Lip

Thumbhole behind

Barrel

Foot

It is always advisable to have expert advice in the selection of an instrument. Although the recorder is relatively inexpensive, careful selection is still necessary. Recorders are made of plastic or wood.

Plastic recorders are breakable, but with reasonable care will last a lifetime. Wooden recorders are less vulnerable and tend to have a more mellow tone, but they require careful drying out after playing otherwise moisture expands the wood, distorting the tuning and perhaps eventually splitting the wood.

The tone quality should be clear and pure, without woolliness and breathiness.

It should be easy to play and require very little breath.

Some recorders are made in three pieces instead of two so that the 'foot' can be turned round to fit the little finger. If you are buying a two-piece instrument, be sure you can cover the lowest holes comfortably with the little finger of your right hand.

CARE OF THE RECORDER

Recorders are made in two or three pieces—the mouthpiece, the barrel with the finger holds, and, if in three parts, a movable foot. These parts should be separated carefully after playing by using a screwing movement. Then the instrument should be cleaned and dried with a mop specially designed for the purpose or by pulling a piece of soft, absorbent rag through it. Wooden recorders should be played for only short periods when they are new. Gradually they will become 'played in' sufficiently to be used for long periods. Do not attempt to clean the wind-way or the lip of a recorder with any-thing hard. It is usually sufficient to place a finger over the window and blow sharply through the wind-way to clear it of accumulated moisture. Use a feather to remove any specks of dirt.

After a time the joints become rather loose. If the lapping is made of waxed thread, scratch it a little with the thumb nail to tighten it.

Lappings made of cork or composition material usually become very tight. They can be lightly sandpapered and rubbed with cork grease or lanoline.

If a firm case is made for a recorder there is far less chance of it breaking.

MUSIC STANDS

A music stand suitable for use on a table or desk can be made very easily. Take two pieces of firm cardboard or heavy manilla paper 35 cm × 25 cm and join them together with a firm binding of linen tape or sellotape along one of the long edges. To ensure easy folding the pieces of cardboard should be 6 mm apart when bound.

Attach the two ends of a piece of tape about 23 cm long to the centre of the two long sides. This will make a tent-like stand that can be folded flat. With two plastic clothes pegs the music can be clipped to the sides of the stand to prevent it from sliding. Music can be kept inside the stand when not in use.

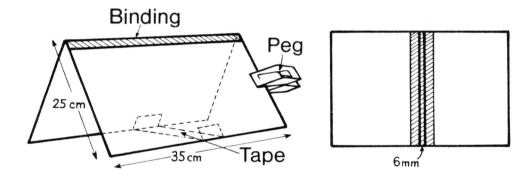

MUSIC READING

The old-fashioned method of learning to read words was to learn letter by letter—C-A-T, cat; D-O-G, d g; and so on. Modern methods are directed toward recognition of words as a whole without first analysing them into letters; indeed towards recognition of whole sentences such as 'Run to the door'. Later, separate words and then letters are distinguished. Similarly, in music individual notes should not be learnt in isolation but in musical phrases. New notes and notes of differing length should be learnt in groups and in relation to other notes already known. The method outlined in this book encourages the reading of groups of notes and whole phrases at a time in order to express musical ideas.

TIME VALUES

This phrase method of learning to read music is particularly useful in reading time values. To know that two quavers equal one crotchet or four semi-quavers is no guarantee that you understand the relative time value of the notes in time patterns such as:

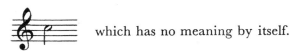

Try to recognise such phrases as a whole and feel the basic rhythm underlying them. Feel each bar of music moving towards the end of the phrase and each phrase linked to other phrases in the melody. Similarly in learning notation it is not enough to learn

which has no meaning by itself.

Learn the C in relation to other notes already known, e.g.

In this way groups of notes are recognised at a glance as a shape rather than as C, B, C, A, or C, B, A, G.

It is as unwise in music as in anything else to try to learn more than one new thing at a time. Each new note and each new time value should be practised in relation to what is already known. In this book the tunes are most carefully graded so that a good deal of practice is given to each new point. This important consideration will limit the tunes chosen to the range of notes and to time values which have already been learned.

To play well at sight on any instrument you need to recognise note and time patterns at a glance and to translate these automatically into muscular responses. These automatic reactions are acquired by interested practice and repetition. Suggestions are given in this book for additional activities for this purpose.

Achievement is the greatest practice incentive. With the recorder the first lesson brings the achievement of playing tunes on three notes. After subsequent lessons more varied tunes can be played within the range of notation and time values already learnt. Once all the notes have been learnt, the recorder is as difficult to play well as any other musical instrument, for success depends not only on a high degree of technical skill but also on musicianship and a growing understanding of music. Merely to play the correct notes is of little musical value. The spirit and character of the music are the intangible things that can't be printed. Like a play that needs to be produced, written music needs to be interpreted with thought and care. The chief value in learning to play a recorder is that it can give great satisfaction and enjoyment to students at all stages of development and be a means of expressing feelings and ideas through music.

CLASS WORK

A Note to Teachers

In recorder class work the aim is to establish a little at a time and to find ways of repetition without boredom. New notes or new time values are introduced one by one. To assimilate each new point, pupils should be given plenty of time and varied practice. New material is introduced when that already learned can be read fluently.

Size of Class: A large class of beginners is as manageable as a small class provided the teacher insists on disciplined playing in instruction periods. When the teacher is explaining a point the recorders should be held under the armpit 'to keep the head warm'. This prevents a lot of unnecessary and annoying blowing and leaves the hands free for clapping the time patterns.

Holding the Recorder: The first five notes are played with the left hand only. While they are being learned the recorder is best supported by resting the narrow end in a V made between the first and second fingers of the right hand. The *back* of the hand should be facing the player. In the initial lessons players quickly tire of supporting the recorder with the right hand and tend to cover the lower holes with the fingers. If the back of the supporting hand is facing the player, relaxed fingers will not cover the holes.

Interchange of Hands: Some children tend to make the mistake of playing B-A-G with the fingers of the right hand, and then try to play the lower notes with the left. This leads to difficulty with the bottom hole, which in the Schott recorder can be played only with the little finger of the right hand. Pupils who find it difficult to change to the correct position could play a Dolmetsch or a Dulcet recorder in which the bottom section can be twisted to the left. But the difficulty can be avoided if teachers insist in the first lesson that all pupils play the upper notes with the left hand.

Three Important Points: By systematic practice, aim at these three things:
1. Sure fingering
2. Correct tongueing
3. Quick recognition of notation and time values

SURE FINGERING

Initial Exercise: Cover the hole at the back of the recorder with the left-hand thumb and support the recorder as suggested above.

1. Do not blow, but with flat first finger practise tapping smartly over the hole nearest the mouthpice. Do this until you hear a faint note.
2. Keeping your *first finger down,* tap with the second finger over the second hole.
3. Keeping your *first and second fingers down,* tap with the third finger over the third hole.

Listen for the difference in each sound. Repeat to a time pattern. Players can listen to each other tapping four times on each hole and can keep a watch for fingers that lift when they should be down.

Now tap them once each. Can you hear 'Three Blind Mice'?

The same fingering spells B, A, G.

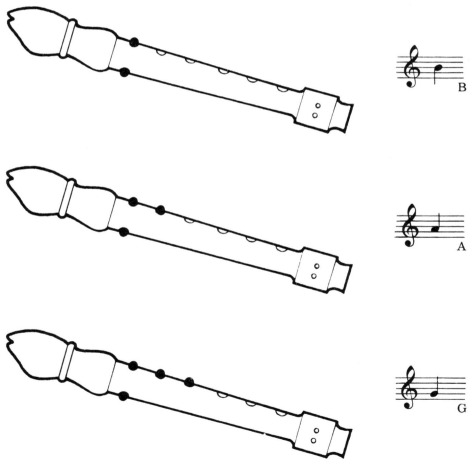

Ways of Repeating Exercise: Put your fingers where they should be for G, B, A. What letter am I fingering? Ask children to demonstrate.

4. Keeping the first finger down, practise tapping with the second and third fingers together from B to G.
5. Press fingers over the holes; look for the bumps on the pads (not on the points) of your fingers.

If all this preliminary work is well done there should not be a chaotic mixture of sounds when playing begins.

CORRECT TONGUEING

Say in the time of 'Three Blind Mice', d, d, d, as softly as possible. Whisper it almost inaudibly.

Put your fingers on your recorder for B. Put the mouthpiece on your lower lip; close your upper lip over it, making sure no air escapes from the sides of your mouth. Now whisper d, d, d into your recorder a number of times until you get a soft, clear note.

Do the same with A and G. Now play the first part of 'Three Blind Mice' (or B, A, G). While some are playing, others can sing the tune right through, or more advanced players can play it on recorders or chime bars.

WHERE TO BREATHE

Most of the tunes in this book are either songs or dance tunes that fall into natural phrases dictated by the words. If you were singing them you would take a breath where the phrases and the sense of the words indicated. When you play them on the recorder you should breathe in exactly the same places.

On pages 22 and 23, 35 and 36, suggested breathing places have been marked with commas to show how to decide where to breathe.

Naturally, when you are learning a tune and playing it slowly you will use more breathing places, but when you can play it up to speed, sing the tune over and phrase it neatly.

THE TUNES

These have been chosen primarily to meet the requirements of a carefully graded learning programme but many of the tunes are familiar folk, hymn and dance tunes still sung in schools. Hymn books and school song-books are usually found in most schools and it should be relatively easy to locate the words of any song wanted for classroom use.

QUICK RECOGNITION OF NOTATION AND TIME VALUES

Notation: Music is written on a five-line staff. Notation can be shown on the fingers, using the left hand as a staff. Imagine your thumb extended to form the top line as in the diagram.

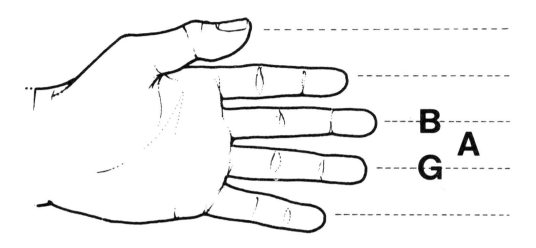

Now show the notes on the staff.

B   A   G   B   A   G

Play tunes from the real staff instead of on the fingers, with a teacher or pupil pointing to the notes.

Time Values: These are best taught from some time pattern already known, e.g.,

(crotchet, minim.)

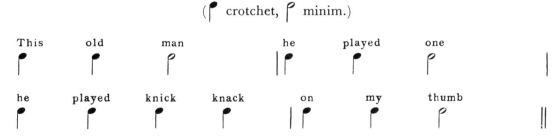

This should be clapped while pupils sing and say 'This old man'.

Now replace words with time names.

ta   ta   ta - a   ta   ta   ta - a   ta   ta   ta   ta   ta   ta   ta - a

Clap these, saying the time names:

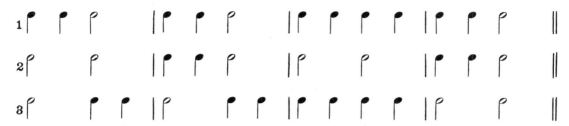

Play these tunes, which have the same time patterns as the examples just practised.

Some of these tunes have only three crotchets $\left(\text{♩}\right)$ in a bar, and use the dotted minim $\left(\text{♩.}\right)$, to which you say T-a-aa, the last 'a' for the dot. Sometimes a crotchet is replaced by a crotchet rest $\left(\text{𝄽}\right)$ —a silence in music. You must count through the rests to keep the time correct. All note values have their corresponding rests which you will learn as the tunes introduce them.

Remember to play softly.

Knocking

A Song (*write your own words*)

Swaying

Long Waltz

School March (o) *semi-breve* (ta-a-a-a)

EAR TRAINING

A Note to Teachers

1. With the three notes B, A and G many tunes can be played. Children and teachers can play their own tunes and have the class echo each phrase, e.g.,

Play a short section at a time. Begin by facing the class, but later let them rely entirely on their ears.

2. A pupil might write a tune on the board while it is being played in sections. It can then be played by the class. At this stage keep within the known notes and time values.

WRITING TUNES

A class can write a tune. Begin by making a four-bar rhythmic pattern on a blank staff and repeat this pattern for the second four bars:

Write A for the last note of bar 4, and G for the last note of bar 8. Fill in the first four bars with any of the notes you know; repeat these for the second four bars. Let the class play this and alter any notes they do not like. Copy this tune on to brown paper and keep it in the class repertoire. When these notes and time values are easily read, move on to new notes.

B

INTRODUCING C

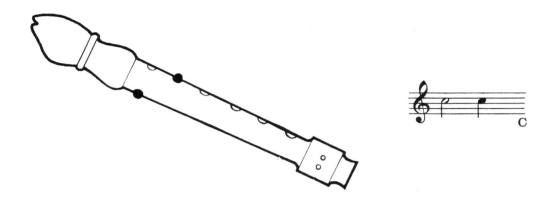

How to Finger C' : Put your fingers as for A; then lift the first finger.
Silent finger practice: A to C'; G to C'; B to C'. This order is important.
Now play each pair of notes three or four times rhythmically, e.g.:

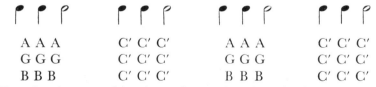

A A A	C' C' C'	A A A	C' C' C'
G G G	C' C' C'	G G G	C' C' C'
B B B	C' C' C'	B B B	C' C' C'

Practise these combinations of notes in other rhythmic patterns.

Stress the Minim

A Walking Tune

Whistling Tune

INTRODUCING D

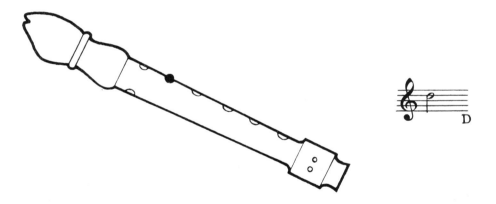

How to Finger D' : Put your fingers as for C' and then take your thumb off the back hole.

Silent finger practice: C to D'; A to D'; G to D'; B to D' several times each in this order.

Now play each pair of notes three or four times in rhythmic patterns as before.

Waltz

19

Rowing

Irish Lullaby

NEW TIME SYMBOL: QUAVER

(two quavers)

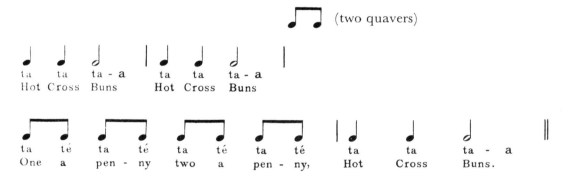

ta   ta   ta - a   ta   ta   ta - a
Hot Cross Buns   Hot Cross Buns

ta té   ta té   ta té   ta té   ta   ta   ta - a
One a pen - ny two a pen - ny, Hot Cross Buns.

Say the time names with the rhythm that you said the words.

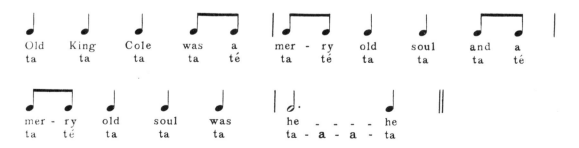

Old   King   Cole   was   a   mer - ry   old   soul   and   a
ta   ta   ta   ta té   ta té ta   ta   ta té

mer - ry old   soul   was   he _ _ _ _ he
ta té ta   ta   ta   ta - a - a - ta

Clap these:

The two dots beside the double bar at the end mean that the section is to be repeated. This sign: ‖ is used often in printed music to save reprinting the parts that are to be played twice. Look out for it in the tunes that follow.

In the next tune you will see the letters D.C. D.C. is short for Da Capo, meaning go back to the beginning. Fine (pronounced fee-nay), means the end.

Go to Sleep Little Brother Peter

INTRODUCING LOW D

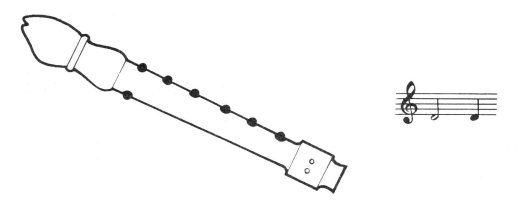

How to Finger Low D: Put the fingers of the left hand as for G. Cover the next three holes with the 1st, 2nd and 3rd fingers of the right hand, and place the right-hand thumb in the most comfortable place under the recorder. Practise tapping with all three fingers of the right hand together.

Silent finger practice: D to G; D to A; D to B; D to C.

Play each pair of notes in rhythmic patterns as before, and also the octave D to D'. Tongue low D very *softly*.

March

Reminders

1. Tongue softly.
2. Introduce each new note with silent finger practice.
3. Continue making up tunes and writing some, using all the notes and time values learned. Make up a gay tune, a sad tune, a march, a dance tune. Tunes need not be written down.
4. Continue ear training as already suggested.
5. Use the recorders for incidental music for classroom plays, mimes, marching, etc., and add tambourines or other percussion instruments as required for the necessary effects.

INTRODUCING A TIE

Sometimes two notes of the same pitch are joined together with a curved line, e.g.:

In this case the second note is not played again. This is just another way of making a note longer. It is used most often when the sound of a note is carried into the next bar, e.g.:

Because you do not play the note again but have to count its time, you leave out the 't' of the time name and say 'a-a' instead of **ta-a**.

INTRODUCING E

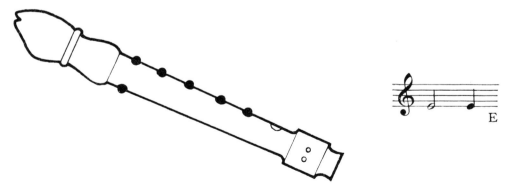

How to Finger E: Put the fingers as for low D and lift the third finger of the right hand.

Silent finger practice: E to D; E to G; E to A; E to B; E to C; and E to D'. Play these pairs of notes in rhythmic patterns as before.

A Sad Song

INTRODUCING F SHARP

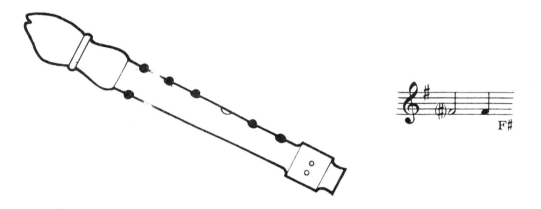

F♯

How to Finger F Sharp: Put the fingers as for low D and lift the first finger of the right hand. The sign ♯ at the beginning of each line of music means that every F is a sharp. Sometimes it is written in this way:

Silent finger practice: F♯ to low D; F♯ to G; F♯ to A; F♯ to B; F♯ to C; F♯ to E. Play these pairs of notes in rhythmic patterns as before.

Oh, No John

Oranges and Lemons

Now the Day is Over

Pop Goes the Weasel

Drink to Me Only

This Old Man

28

NEW TIME SYMBOL: DOTTED CROTCHET

Here is the time pattern of 'God Save the Queen':

Sing through the rest of the National Anthem and you will find that 'victorious', 'glorious', and 'over us' have the same time pattern as 'gracious Queen' and 'noble Queen'.

It might have been written this way. In saying the time name, leave out the 't' as you did for tied notes.

The dot takes the place of the tied note, so it becomes:

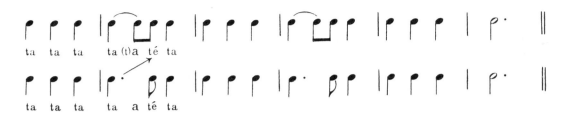

A Dutch Carol

O Come, All Ye Faithful

The Keeper

Melody from Choral Symphony (Beethoven)

CHARACTER IN MUSIC

By now you are probably playing quite fluently, but perhaps the tunes sound rather lifeless and stilted. The phrases in music should swing along in the same way as sentences in speech.

Do the waltzes swing along and make you want to dance?

Ask someone to march to your playing till you both feel 'in step'. You may be playing too quickly or too slowly, or without the swing that carries a tune along. Experiment till you get it. Listen to recordings of bands playing marches and orchestras playing waltzes.

Gentlemen of England

O Worship the King

Tone Quality

While fluency in reading is the main aim at this stage, it is worth while to play the familiar tunes not only for fun but with an ear for the tone quality produced. Do you
1. play without squeaks?
2. play without harshness or 'stringy' tone?
3. think this sounds like a march? etc.

Experiment with pleasant and unpleasant sounds in playing the same tune. Listen to other players if you are playing in a group and ask the others to listen critically to your playing.

AURAL TRAINING

Note to Teachers

Playing by ear is fun and excellent aural training. From the beginning children can repeat by ear a phrase of three notes played by the teacher or another pupil. Use only the known notes. At a later stage many tunes with time values too difficult for reading can be taught by ear in this way. The exercise can be varied by asking pupils to write down the notes played. 'Spelling' is good aural training. One pupil plays a word, the rest write down; e.g., DAD, DEAD, BEAD.

With the complete scale of seven letters many words and some groups of words are possible; e.g., A BAD CABBAGE.

IMPROVISATION

You will enjoy making up tunes on your recorder. If you want music for a special purpose such as a march for assembly, incidental music for a play or puppet play, dance music, or suitable music to accompany a mime, then make it yourself. The music need not be written down unlees you want to keep it for further use.

MUTING THE RECORDER

The continual sound of recorders may become disturbing to other classes and teachers. In most schools there need to be periods of strict silence for recorders. It is an advantage if pupils can sometimes play with a muted tone. A mute is made very simply by cutting a piece of thin card or thin celluloid a little narrower than the window in width and about $3\frac{1}{2}$cm long. Bend over about 1cm at one end and hook into the window. The amount of muting depends on the width of the card and the length of the hook.

Use a rubber band to keep the mute on the recorder when not in use.

c

CLASS PROJECT

Find as many tunes as possible that use the notes learned. Copy them out. Where to look:

(a) Hymn Books
(b) Books of Folk Songs and National Songs
(c) Radio and Television Booklets
(d) Books of Community Songs
(e) Pop songs and tunes from current musicals. They may need to be transposed into the key of G.

Do not attempt to hurry on to new notes. At this stage you are often tempted to learn just one more note that comes into a tune you like or happens to be in the Radio and Television Book. In looking for tunes to play, list any that use 'just one more note', and make a note of it in this textbook for handy, future reference.

SOME HIGHER NOTES

The notes above D are known as 'pinched notes because they are played with the thumb nail of the left hand pushed into the hole at the back. Instead of covering it completely, this leaves a little of the hole open—about one-quarter.

It is a good plan to practise sliding the thumb nail in and over the hole with as little movement as possible. Just bend and straighten the upper joint of the thumb. If you can do this the upper notes are quite easy.

INTRODUCING UPPER E

How to Finger Upper E: Finger as for lower E and pinch the hole at the back:

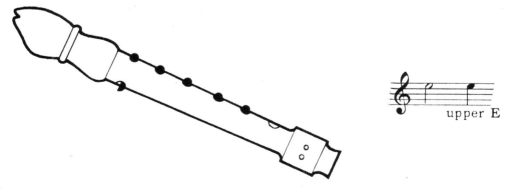

upper E

You will need to blow a little differently for 'pinched' notes. Experiment until you get a clear, but not shrill, sound.

Silent finger practice: E′ — E; E′ — A; E′ — C′; E′ — D′.
Now play the same groups to a rhythmic pattern.

35

Sweet Nightingale

God Save the Queen

INTRODUCING UPPER G

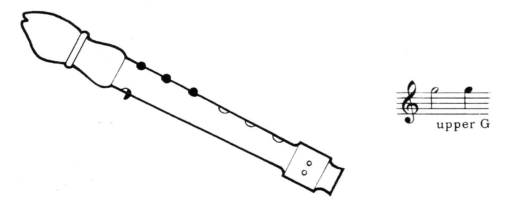

upper G

How to Finger Upper G: Finger as for lower G and 'pinch' the hole at the back.

Silent finger practice: G′ — E′; G′ — G; G′ — D; G′ — C′; G′ — D′.
Now play the same groups to a rhythmic pattern.

A March

NEW SIGNS

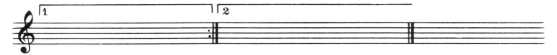

To save space, music to be repeated is not written twice. You will remember the repeat sign is two dots before a double bar. Sometimes the last bar of the first time through is different from the second time through. When that happens space is saved by writing the two bars and putting the sign 1st and 2nd above the bar, e.g.:

You play 1st time bar the first time and replace it by 2nd time bar in the repeat. Some of the tunes in the next section use these signs.

INTRODUCING UPPER F SHARP

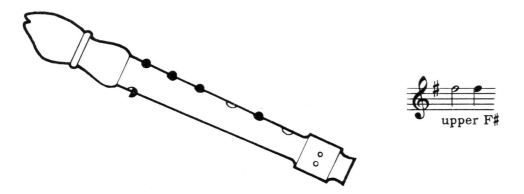

upper F♯

How to Finger Upper F♯: Finger as for lower F♯, 'pinch' the hole at the back, and raise the third finger of your right hand.

Silent finger practice: F♯′ — G′; F♯′ — E′ F♯′ — F♯; F♯′ — D′; F♯′ — B.
Now play the same groups to a rhythmic pattern.

Turn Ye to Me

Rufty Tufty

The Girl I Left Behind Me

Furry Day Carol

38

Early One Morning

COMPOUND TIME

Compound Time is easily recognised by time signatures with 6, 9 or 12 as the upper figure, e.g.:

6	12	9	6	9	12
8	8	8	16	16	16

The time most often used in folk songs is 6/8.

Say the words of these rhymes in the usual rhythms and you will be interpreting the time symbols correctly.

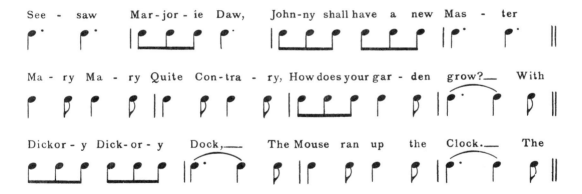

These notes represent the speech rhythms you find you use naturally for these rhymes.

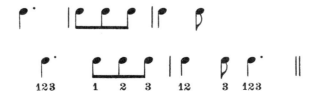

39

You should learn to recognise each *group* of notes as part of the rhythmic pattern. French time names of Mary, Mary:

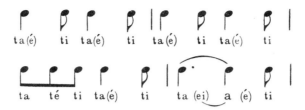

ta(é)   ti   ta(é)   ti   ta(é)   ti   ta(é)   ti

ta   té   ti   ta(é)   ti   ta (ei)   a (é)   ti

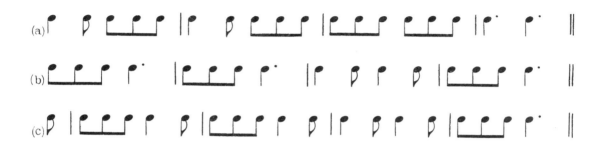

(a)

(b)

(c)

1. See - saw Mar-jor - ie Daw, John-ny shall have a new mas - ter.

2. Dick-or - y Dick-or - y Dock,__ The mouse ran up the clock.__ The

clock struck one and down the mouse ran, Dick-or - y Dick-or - y Dock.__

3. Ma - ry. Ma - ry, quite con-tra - ry, How does your gar-den grow?

40

English Folk Song *(Farmer's Daughter)*

Dashing away with a Smoothing Iron

MORE ABOUT COMPOUND TIME

In some tunes this 𝄽 is altered a little to look like this 𝄽

It is like this in 'Silent Night'

Si - - lent night,   Ho - - ly night   Ho - ly In - fant so ten - der and mild

and in 'Skye Boat Song'.

Car - ry the lad that's born to be king, O - ver the sea to Skye.

Try these:

Skye Boat Song

Fine

D.C.

Sellengers Round

Part Two

★

You have now learned to use these notes:

Most of the pieces you have been playing have been in the key of G major. You will have noticed this sign 𝄞# at the beginning of the pieces. It is one way of showing that the melody is probably in G major. There are other keys to be used if G major is not the best key. It may be too high or too low for some pieces. Some keys are better than others for recorder playing. D major is a good one.

From this point on new notes will be introduced as new keys are used.

THE KEY OF D MAJOR

When you play in D major, C♯ as well as F♯ must be used. The sign at the beginning of the music looks like this 𝄞## and this note 𝄞## ♪ is C♯.

How to Finger C♯: Put the fingers as they would be for A; then uncover the thumb hole at the back.

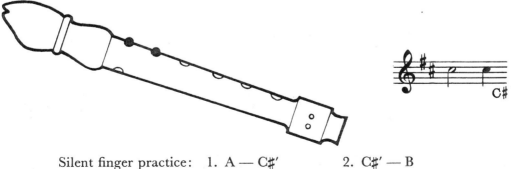

Silent finger practice: 1. A — C♯'   2. C♯' — B
                              3. C♯' — E   4. C♯' — E'
Play the same groups rhythmically, using the new time values.

43

The Lorelei

Star of Donegal

Barcarolle (*Offenbach*)

SLURRING

With woodwind instruments much of the character and variety in the music is introduced by slurring two or more notes. So far you have been 'tongueing' every note.
Most notes are tongued, and that is why much practice must be given to good articu-
lation. Now is the time to introduce an occasional slur. Instead of tongueing each note
in a group covered by a slur, tongue the first only; in the first bar of Ex. 1 below, the
first two notes are slurred and the other two tongued.

Practise saying 'too-oo' for two notes slurred or 'too-oo-oo' for three, and so on.
Some fingerings are easily slurred while others are difficult. In the following exercises
you will find those which are harder for you. Give them plenty of practice.

THE KEY OF C MAJOR

There are no signs at the beginning for C major. All notes are 'natural', that is, not sharps or flats. In this key F is natural, not sharp as in the previous pieces.

How to Finger F: Cover all the holes on your recorder, then lift the second finger of your right hand.

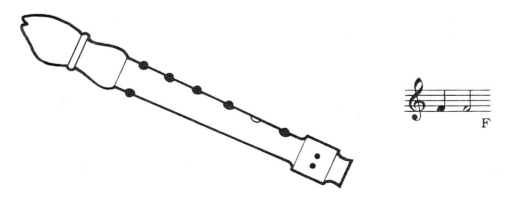

Now play F to G. This is tricky. You have to lift the first, third and fourth fingers of the right hand together.

Silent finger practice: A — F; B — F; C' — F; D' — F.

Now play the same groups to a rhythmic pattern.

My Bonnie

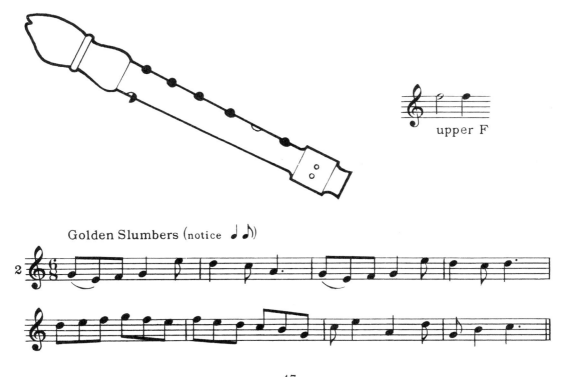

How to Finger Upper F: Finger as for lower F, pinch the hole at the back and lift the little finger of your right hand.

upper F

Golden Slumbers (notice ♩ ♪)

Song of Western Men *(Simple time again)*

Minuet (Purcell)

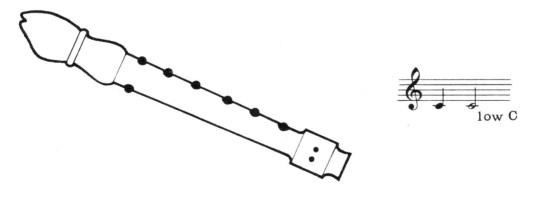

How to Finger Low C: Cover all the holes on your recorder and blow very, very gently.

low C

The best exercise for getting low C is to play low F, then cover the remaining open hole with the second finger of the right hand. Try it many times.

Silent finger practice: F — C; E — C; G — C; C' — C.

Silent Night

5

THE KEY OF F MAJOR

One way of recognising the key of F major is to find one flat (one ♭ sign) in the key signature. The sign is written with the middle line of the staff cutting through it, e.g.,

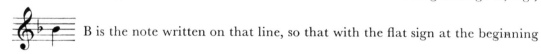 B is the note written on that line, so that with the flat sign at the beginning of each line every B in the music will be B flat (B♭).

How to Finger B♭: Put down your fingers as for G, then raise the middle finger. Now add only the first finger of your right hand.

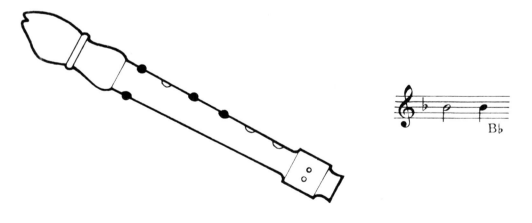

49

As an accidental it looks like this:
The B marked with an * is B natural.

O Can Ye Sew Cushions

INTRODUCING RESTS

The quaver rest.

The dotted crotchet rest.

The crotchet rest.

Rests used in compound time to replace note values where a silence is required, e.g.:
The curved ⌒ indicates the number of notes replaced.

You think or whisper the rest beat or, if you are clapping the time, gently tap the desk when there is a rest. It is all too easy to ignore rests. Try these:

In Dulce Jubilo

Scottish Tune

NEW TIME SYMBOLS: SEMI-QUAVERS

Here are three that you will often see:

four semi-quavers (tafa téfé);

a quaver and two semi-quavers (ta téfé);

a dotted quaver and one semi-quaver (ta-fi).

Did-dle did-dle dump-ling my son John   Went to bed with his stock-ings on.
ta - fa té-fé ta   té ta té ta   ta - fi ta-té fé ta té ta.

Say the time names in the same rhythm as you said the words.

The 'Keel Row' uses this one

'Piper of Galway' uses this one

'Jingle Bells' uses [symbol] and [symbol]

'Silent Worship' and 'The Weggis Song' use

The Keel Row

52

Piper of Galway

Jingle Bells

Fine Verse

D.C.

British Grenadiers

53

These tunes use the time symbols and keys that you know. Look carefully to see if there are flats or sharps to play, and get the rhythm in your mind before you begin playing.

God Defend New Zealand

Silent Worship (Handel)

The Weggis Dance

Irish Washerwoman

All Things Bright and Beautiful

TIME PATTERNS

Note to Teachers

The quick recognition of time patterns is as essential for fluent reading of music as is the quick recognition of words in reading sentences. Teachers might use flash cards as a method of training the pupils to grasp a complete bar at a glance. A good size for a flash card is 10 cm by 30 cm. This is big enough for one bar. The noteheads should be ovals about 2 cm long, and the stems and other lines 3 to 6 mm. A 'felt pen' is useful for drawing notes; so is a sharpened stick dipped in indian ink. Time patterns should be written with careful spacing since the eye takes in groups correctly spaced more quickly than irregular patterns. Flash cards of the time patterns suggested below are well worth preparing. They can be used in all classes for years.

The aim of using the flash cards is to accustom the children to reading whole bars at a glance without having to analyse out the separate notes, in the same way that they recognise a word or phrase at a glance without spelling out the separate letters. Expose the card for a few seconds and ask the children to tap or say or play the time pattern they have seen. Repeat the pattern several times on a sequence of notes, e.g., G, A, B, A, G. Gradually reduce the time the card is exposed until the whole time pattern is recognised in a flash.

When one bar of music is easily grasped at a glance, increase to two bars. When you make two-bar flash cards it is important that the second bar should be mostly like the first, as in the examples 1-5 below. Later, alter one group only in the second bar (6-9). This method encourages the eye to spot the difference between the bars.

Most people tend to be uncertain about time, either in singing or in playing an instrument. Frequent informal practice on time patterns with flash cards is a great help to them. They can be used in a variety of ways: the children can clap them, say their time names, use percussion instruments, sing them, write them down from memory, imitate them from each other, or use them as tongueing practice on the recorder. It is a pleasant variant to have the time patterns played on two or three notes of a chord. Patterns such as these could be used:

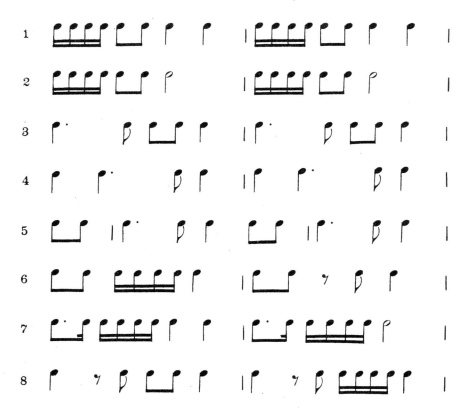

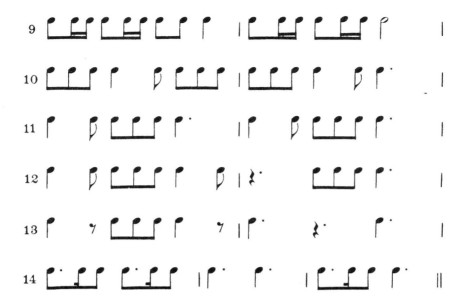

SUGGESTIONS FOR WRITING TUNES

Note to Teachers

You now have many notes, rests and several keys with which you are familiar. Use some of these time patterns for a tune: e.g. No. 9.

Or make it into 4 bars by adding two more at the beginning.

THE KEY OF B FLAT MAJOR

You know that one flat in the key signature indicates the key of F major. When there are two flats in the key signature the key is B♭ major. Both the B and E are flattened.

How to Finger Upper E♭: Open the hole at the back, put down the second and third fingers of the left hand, and the first, second, and third fingers of the right hand.

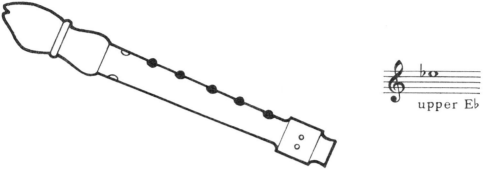

upper E♭

Silent finger practice D′ — E♭′; E′ — E♭′; F′ — E♭′.

How to Finger Lower E♭: Put your fingers on your recorders as you would for lower D, now slide the third finger of right hand back a little until one of the small holes is uncovered.

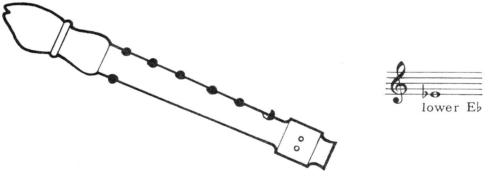

lower E♭

Silent finger practice: D — E♭; G — E♭; F — E♭.

A Hymn

58

THE PAUSE

A new sign

In the next tune you will see the new sign ⌢ over two notes. The sign is called a pause mark and indicates that you hold the note longer than the note value. You decide just how long. Sing the tune to find out how long the pause should be.

Sweet Lass of Richmond Hill

A Round

Blow the Wind Southerly

A Hymn

5

THE KEY OF A MINOR

Composers know the limitations of the instruments for which they write. When too many flats and sharps are used in music for recorders, the fingering becomes complicated. It is usual, therefore, to use the keys already learnt: C major, G major, D major, F major, and B♭ major, and the minor keys which use these key signatures.

So far, only major keys have been used. Play this tune:

It sounds a little different from the tunes you have been playing. This is in a minor key. The key note is A, not C, as you would expect where there are no flats or sharps in the key signature. All minor keys have another sharp or natural that is not written into the key signature. It is always the leading note, that is, the note below the key note, that is affected. In A minor it is G sharp.

How to Finger Lower G♯:
Cover the hole at the back and first and second in each hand.

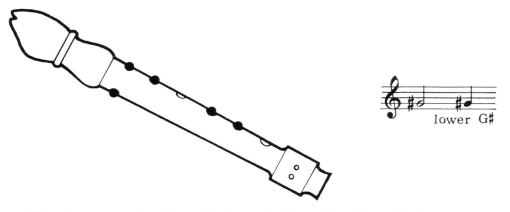

lower G♯

Silent finger practice: G♯ — A; G♯ — B; G♯ — C♯'; G♯ — E'; E'; G♯ — F♯.

How to Finger Upper G♯:

Notice that in *upper G* you pinch the hole at the back and use *only the first finger* of the right hand instead of first and second as in lower G♯.

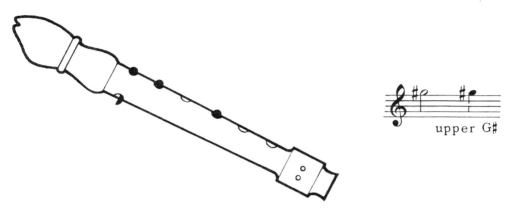

upper G♯

Silent finger practice: G♯′ — G♯; G♯′ — E′; G♯′ — C♯′.

Greensleeves

Air (Purcell)

How to Finger Upper A: Upper A is the same as lower A but for the pinched hole at the back.

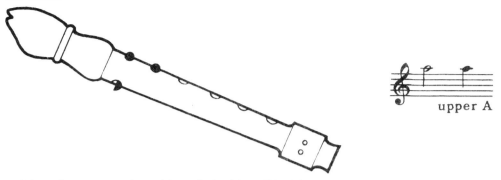

upper A

Silent finger practice: A′ — G♯′; A′ — G′; A′ — A.

Hiking

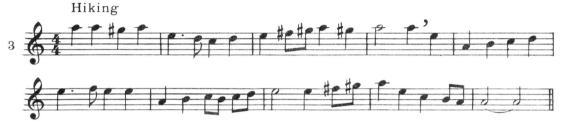

THE KEY OF E MINOR

The key of E minor uses the same key signature as G major, i.e., one sharp and the extra sharp is D♯.

How to Finger Upper D♯:

Open the hole at the back and cover second and third of the left hand and the first, second, and third of the right hand.

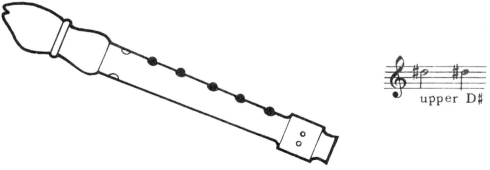

upper D♯

Silent finger practice: D♯′ — E′; D♯′ — D′; D♯′ — C♯′.

How to Finger Lower D♯:

Place your fingers as for lower D and slide your third finger of the right hand until one small hole is uncovered.

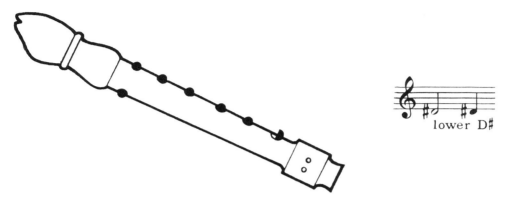

lower D♯

Silent finger practice: D♯ — D; D♯ — E; D♯ — F♯.

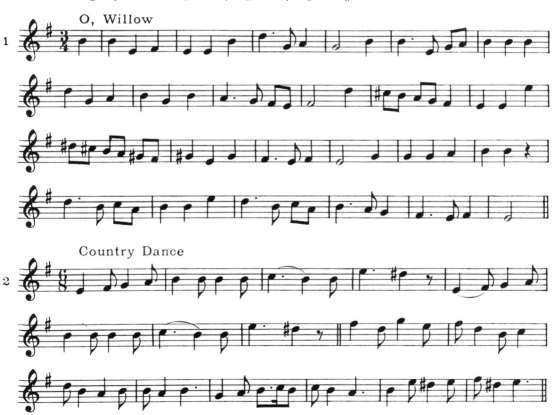

1 O, Willow

2 Country Dance

Gavotte

Did you notice that D♯ and E♭ were the same? They are the same note on a recorder, but are written differently to suit the key the music is written in. All notes have more than one name.

You now know that D♯ is also E♭. Notice that the flat name is one letter name higher than the sharp name. Therefore:

C♯ is also D♭.   A♯ is also B♭.

D♯ is also E♭.   F♯ is also G♭.

G♯ is also A♭.

You know all these notes. (Play games to give practice in alternative names.)

THE KEY OF B MINOR

In B minor the key signature is the same as for D major: two sharps. The extra sharp is A♯ (same fingering as for B♭).

Country Dance

Coventry Carol

God Rest You Merry, Gentlemen

To finger high B, see page 67.

THE KEY OF D MINOR

The key signature for D minor is the same as for F major, i.e., one flat. The accidental or extra sharp is C#.

Miller of Dee

E

Down among the Dead Men

THE KEY OF G MINOR

The key signature for G minor is the same as for B♮ major, i.e., two flats. The accidental is F♯.

A Round

Old King Cole

SOME UPPER NOTES

Some of these notes are not used often. They require a lot of practice and experiment to be played clearly. You may need to look up the fingering as required. Here are some exercises to help you to learn them.

How to Finger High B♭: Pinch the hole at the back and cover first and second holes of left hand and second and third holes of the right hand.

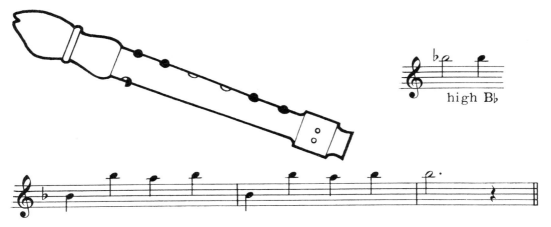

high B♭

How to Finger High B: Pinch the hole at the back and cover holes with first and second fingers of both hands.

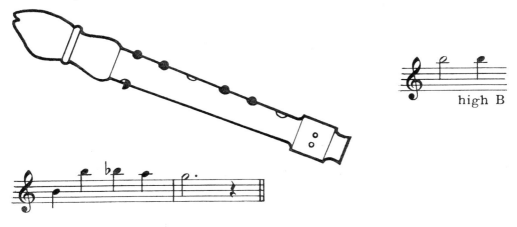

high B

How to Finger High C: Pinch the hole at the back and cover the first hole for the left hand and the first and second holes for the right hand.

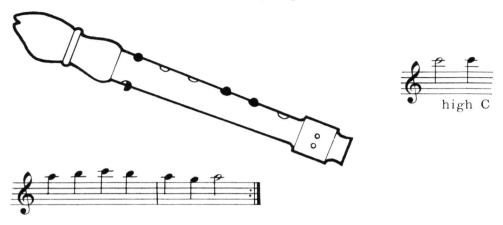

high C

How to Finger High D: Pinch the hole at the back and cover first and third holes for both right and left hands.

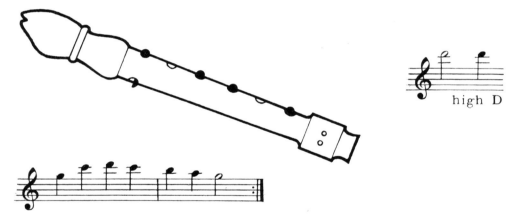

high D

If you have much difficulty in getting a clear note, decrease or increase the amount of open space in the 'pinched hole'. The *thumb nail* controls the opening. Try to concentrate air going into the recorder into a very thin stream. This helps to give clear top notes.

Here are some first tunes transposed up an octave to give you some practice on higher notes.

INTERPRETATION

The playing of notes in time does not make music any more than just speaking words can make a story. When you talk or tell a story you stress the important words and phrases and you hold your listener's attention by building up to the point or the climax of the story; the same applies to music. When you sing, you find that the words usually fit the musical phrases; therefore you sing in phrases, and each phrase has its most important word or note, and each phrase leads on to the next. Music, like speech, is made up of phrases and sentences, and like speech it is only when these phrases are put together and lead from one to another that the music has any meaning. You can play all the notes on the recorder and understand time values, but you will not be making music until you think the notes into phrases and make each phrase interesting and meaningful.

It is difficult to explain how this is done, but here are some suggestions to help you look for the meaning in music. Meaning can be found in two of the essential elements of music—*Rhythm* and *Melody*.

Let's look for it first in the Rhythm. A composer has to work within the conventions that make the reading of music possible. He can put down time values such as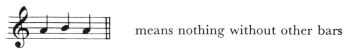

and he has to arrange these symbols within bars that usually contain the same number of beats. That is as near as he can get to giving us the *rhythm* (which is the way these time values sweep along from bar to bar until they reach the end of a phrase), and it is the player's job to read into these time values and bar lines what the composer really means. Just as 'is' means nothing without other words around it, so

means nothing without other bars

around it.

A sentence such as 'Mary "is" playing her recorder' gives 'is' a meaning. And a musical phrase such as

gives  a meaning.

The arrows below show just where the sentence or musical phrase is going.

Very often tunes are written with musical phrases of four bars, but of course that is not always so. Here is the time pattern for a tune which has a four-bar phrase followed by a six-bar phrase to make up the whole sentence:

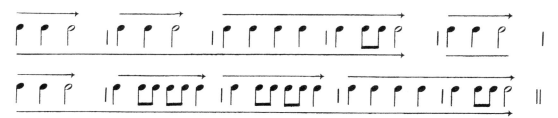

Notice the lines underneath leading to the end of the sentence marked with an arrowhead. However, within these long phrases there can be further musical ideas. Notice that in the first four bars the first two are alike. They could mean something like this 'Don't do that. Don't do that. Don't do that or I shall smack.'

Below are printed six tunes in which the phrases have been marked with straight lines and with arrowheads to show the ends of the phrases. Where the lines dip making a V, it means that the bars sweep on and on like a ball bouncing until they reach the end of the phrase.

It should be remembered that there are often several possible interpretations of a piece of music. If you try to play a tune in several ways you are more likely to find the composer's meaning. Whenever you play, mean something; if it is clear in your mind it will be clear to the listener.

71

Sing the above musical phrases over, feeling each note moving towards the end of each phrase marked by the arrow. Try to forget the bar lines within the phrase. They tend to prevent you from seeing the whole musical phrase.

Play the melody now thinking about the phrases. When an idea is repeated in music it either emphasises the idea or echoes it. You must decide by trial which you think it is and play it in that way.

When you have the phrases clearly decided, look for the most important note in each phrase, that is, the climax of the phrase. In speech we never stress 'and', 'the', 'of', 'to' and such words, but skip over them towards the important words. Say 'Try to forget bar lines' as you would normally, then say it stressing each word evenly. Notice the difference. In musical sentences you do the same. Here is an example:

The recorder has its own problems of interpretation. You cannot alter the volume of the sound very much without altering the pitch. On some instruments you can emphasise the repeated sections by playing them more loudly. On a recorder you must give the impression of more volume by sustaining the notes a little longer than you would for very soft playing. Similarly you can get an echo by making the notes very, very short.

When you listen to the radio, listen particularly to the phrasing of instrumentalists such as violinists and flautists. You will notice that they make their music interesting by playing in phrases which move forward in a rhythmic flow. Look over the tunes you play and try to make out their musical sense. If you have a friend who has had some musical training, ask for some help in interpretation and you will find playing much more interesting.

Long notes and tied notes are more difficult to play. Always decide whether they are leading towards the important notes in the phrase, or away from it. If they are leading towards the important notes they must give the impression of getting stronger but if they follow the important notes they must appear to fade with the tapering of the phrase ending, e.g.:

PHRASED TUNES

Come Lasses and Lads

ORNAMENTS

Various writers interpret musical ornaments in different ways and composers in different periods have intended different effects by the same symbols. You can read about this in *The Interpretation of Music*, by Thurston Dart. The following suggestions are made as a guide to recorder players:

A few simple ornaments can be used with discretion to colour and decorate an otherwise simple melody. Those in common use are the trill, the closed trill, the mordent, the acciaccatura, the turn, the coulé, and the appoggiatura.

(*a*) All ornaments should begin on the beat.

(*b*) All ornaments should be played as fast as possible.

(*c*) All ornaments, except the mordent, should begin on the note above.

The Trill: Shown 'tr' above a note.

(*a*) *Cadential Trill* (marking the ends of musical phrases):

1. Begin on the note above and hold it for half the time value of the note.
2. Trill between note above and note itself for the second half of the beat and finish on the note itself.
3. Make a momentary pause before playing the next note.
   e.g.:

Whether the movement is fast or slow, the trill is played as fast as possible. The number of notes in the trill depends on the speed of movement. If it is very quick only three will be possible. The time value will determine the number. If the note to be trilled is dotted, begin on the note above and hold it either one-third or two-thirds of the time value according to the harmony, and then trill the remaining two-thirds or one-third.

(*b*) *Passing Trills* (shown 'tr' above a note).

Trills at other than cadence points are called passing. Trills begin on the note above and are played as fast as possible within the given note value.

(*c*) *Closed Trills* (⌇⌇⌇) Play four notes—note above, note itself, note above, note itself, holding the last note for the remainder of the time value.

written   played

Coulé: A coulé is either written in full in the music or left to the discretion of the performer, e.g.:

These are very small notes.

The small notes make up the coulé. They are two notes preceding the given note, either above or below it. Begin the coulé *on* the beat, not before it. You can introduce this ornament at your own discretion.

In older music, ornaments were left to the performer to add and were not indicated by the composer. They are often introduced when the tune leaps from a lower to a higher note, as in the following tune, e.g.:

Those marked X were added to this melody.

The Mordent (✦) is always inverted, that is, the note itself, the note below, the note itself, e.g.:

Play the first two notes as fast as possible and hold the third for the remainder of the time value.

The Turn (∞), as its shape suggests, is: note above, note itself, note below, note itself.

Appoggiatura

The small notes take half the value of the notes they precede. Early music used the appoggiatura, but nowadays the time values are written as they are played.

Acciaccatura

Note the difference. The small notes have lines through their stems and are played as fast as possible and, as always, on the beat.

PLAYING OTHER RECORDERS

Much of the enjoyment in playing recorders is in being able to play any part whether for descant, treble, tenor, or bass. Most recorder players have at least two instruments. Now that you can play a descant you will find you can play the tenor. The fingering and reading of the notation is exactly the same. The space between the holes is much wider, but you soon become used to stretching your fingers to cover the holes.

The treble recorder is in many ways the most satisfying to play. The tone quality is pleasant, and there is a wide selection of interesting music written for treble recorders, either solo or in consort. To play the treble you will need to learn the difference in notation for the fingering that corresponds to that you have learnt for the descant; e.g., the fingering for

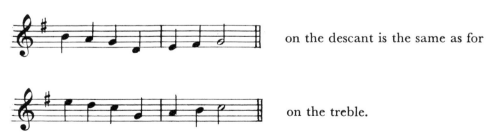

on the descant is the same as for

on the treble.

This may seem confusing and difficult at first, but you will be surprised how quickly you learn it. As the fingering for the sopranino and bass recorders is the same as for the treble, you will then be able to play all five instruments of the recorder family.

TABLE OF FINGERINGS FOR THE RECORDER

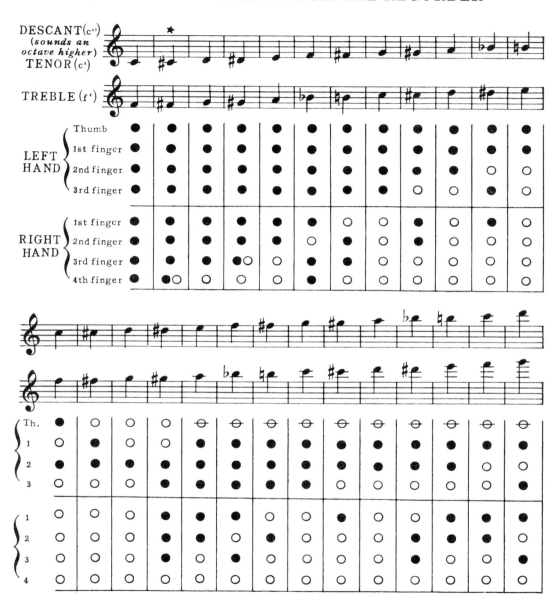

*This note cannot be played on a tenor with single key for the lowest hole.

SOME EXCEPTIONAL FINGERING

For shakes:

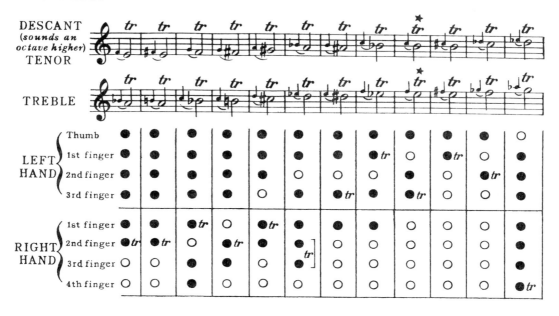

NOTE

When starting a shake on the upper note, it is generally best to use the normal fingering for that note before going into the shake fingering.

* This fingering gives a useful alternative for legato passages where the b (descant) or c (treble) is unaccented.

MUSIC FOR RECORDERS

At this stage you will need plenty of new music. There is a large repertoire of interesting, well graded, and inexpensive music available for recorder players.

Ask your music dealer for catalogues of recorder music published by various music publishers.

The music is listed under headings, Solos, Duets, Trios, etc., and the instrument for which each composition is written is indicated. The compositions are graded according to difficulty.

If your music dealer does not stock the music you want he will order it for you.

Index of Tunes

★